Fishing for Light

Prior works in the
Whitebird Chapbook Series:

Trey Moore
we forget we are water
2006

Joseph Trombatore
Screaming at Adam
2007

Sofia Starnes
Corpus Homini
2008

Fishing for Light

Marian Aitches

WingsPress

San Antonio, Texas
2009

Fishing for Light
© 2009 by Marian Aitches

Cover image: "Grandma Ida Mae fishing the Guadalupe."
Photo courtesy of the author

First Edition

ISBN: 978-0-916727-63-5

Wings Press
627 E. Guenther
San Antonio, Texas 78210
Phone/fax: (210) 271-7805

On-line catalogue and ordering:
www.wingspress.com
All Wings Press titles are distributed to the trade by
Independent Publishers Group
www.ipgbook.com

Library of Congress Cataloging-in-Publication Data

Aitches, Marion.
  Fishing for light / Marion Aitches. -- 1st ed.
     p. cm. -- (Whitebird chapbook series; no. 4)
  ISBN 978-0-916727-63-5 (alk.paper)
  I. Title.
  PS3601.I86F57 2009
  811'.6--dc22

Except for fair use in reviews and/or scholarly considerations, no portion of this book may be reproduced in any form without the written permission of the author or the publisher.

*For Grandma and Diane,
born for October*

Contents

In the Stories	1
Remembered	3
A Mother's October	5
Winter Solstice	7
Rivers	9
Fishing for Light	10
At the End	12
Listening to Bach's Art of Fugue	13
Fall in the Hill Country	15
Spelling	16
Bones	17
When Absence is Presence	18
Joy	19
Distances	20
My Last Lithuanian Aunt	21
San Antonio Summer	22
The Painting	23
Grandma's Daughter	24

Double Overtime	25
Winter Roses	27
The Parakeet of Grief	28
Fishing the Last Time	29
White Light	30
Your Baby's Grave	31
Spirit Bundle for Diane	32
In the Mourning Store	34
The Bird's Journey	35
What We Know ...	37
About the Author	38
Acknowledgments	38

In the Stories

I am the tough sister, the one
who saved the others,
the one who stayed awake,
stood in the door, trying
to keep the monster at bay.

In my mother's story, I
am the mother,
first of five, the one who sang
and braided hair,
cooked beans and cornbread
while Mother nursed other children
to pay the bills.

In my father's story, I am Anna, his mother,
the Lithuanian who washed our grandfather's hair
with lye, after she smelled his lover's skin.
She was also the one
whose first boy fell
into a tub of boiling water
on a washday when she was drunk.

I was an angry girl who grew
into a man-eating woman, all of us
crying; but— I am also
Grandma Ida Mae, who stood
on one long left leg, right leg crooked, foot
at the side of her knee, long after eighty.
Leaning her stomach against the sink,
she laughed so hard, throwing her head back
to breathe—a practical woman who kept secrets;
we shared a bowl of hominy soup
or a cup of sassafras tea.

In my story,
she kept me breathing
until I could write
my own history.

Remembered

1.

Just one thing you gotta do in this life,
she'd say, perched
at the wooden table
she painted green.

Die! she'd shout, hiding
a laugh in her mouth.
Grandmaaa— I'd complain.

Naw, she'd protest, clutching her cup
of steaming sassafras tea,
everything else is free.

2.

*Don't worry with stuff that won't
matter later.*

Barely turning her head
away from the stove where she stirred
Cream of Wheat, she'd catch

my whining words: *We broke up* or *I could've
made an A* or *She got the part I wanted*—

Her response, the same. Dark eyes.
—*Who's gonna care after five years?*

3.

Always forgive your enemies.
My sister and I would fight like cats
over one piece of fish. *Kiss each other
good night*, she'd insist.

No, that's not good enough, try again—until
we'd kissed so many times— we laughed in bed,
curling our bodies into warm spoons.

A Mother's October

Now is the time of year
when wind-pushed gold leaves
on chrysanthemum feet moved her
like a boat on a river; she laughed
at life like the dream she wanted
to have before that long-ago

fall when the blunt Texas sky she loved
rushed into their year like a dream
that pushes you cloud-like and leaves
you panting, hard as a child
who has raked all day and moved
piles of pecan leaves into one heap.

Moving slowly now, she remembers
that fall—that day, blue—no one
dreamed it would change forever,
tilt her world askew. Leaves
swirled in wind like eddies in a river,
fell in drifts. The pecan tree sang

to the child who peered down
from the roof, full of flying
dreams—the youngest, the wild one
they all loved the most. Shouting up,
they cautiously moved close to the edge

of the shed. *Careful, don't fall*,
she called, but the child said, *leave me
alone. I'll fly into that pile of leaves,*

land like a bird. She would always
remember that—how reckless

dreams can be. Before the next fall,
she took them all to a treeless place—
desert nights piled within walls
a child could fall safely into. Where
dangerous dreams moved inside.

Winter Solstice

A narrow river. Shallow.
Not fast or slow. Not warm.
Not cold. Clear enough to see

light-colored rocks lining
the sandy bottom. In my
dream I am not running

or even picking a way through
stones not jagged or smooth,
sharp on bare feet from time

to time, navigable
in the even flow. No, in this dream
I am standing

motionless on one long leg,
right foot braced
against left knee.

Like the white heron
at the lily-thick edge
of the San Antonio River,

poised to find minnows
in opaque water.
Like my grandma Ida

in her resting position,
strong brown arm
casting a cane pole
into the muddy waters
of the Guadalupe, head

thrown back laughing
at the crazy blessing:
moonlight in a place
warm enough to fish.

Rivers

I have known the slow Guadalupe—
        childhood picnics—sisters and cousins
          playing tag on grassy banks   littered
            with cane poles, cork and string.

Those days with her at the river—
        Grandma's low voice, quiet gestures—and the earth
        solid under the grass   under the quilt where
            we napped after fishing.

Another Guadalupe too—further east
        near Seguin—where Grandpa built
        the house he'd planned and a swing
            he placed at the river's edge.

We swayed—suspended over water—
        dared each other to jump
        in summer—lying like leaf-covered logs in fall,
            clinging to the wooden slats.

Five years, the river held them together
        before the cancer—the end of Grandpa.
        Afterwards   the flood—
            and the river overflowed Grandma's house

filled with silt—left muddy tracks
        two feet up the wall, furniture ruined on the swollen
        floors of an empty house   she would never
            manage to clean out.

Fishing for Light

> *The present life of man on earth is like*
> *the swift flight of a single sparrow through*
> *the banqueting hall. . . .*
>
> —Venerable Bede (673-735)
>
> *No. We want something more about joy,*
> *more moments loving the light inside*
> *before dark calls the monster into the hall.*

One by one, birds fly through the wide hall—
     shadows on fire-lit walls
     brighter than the night outside.
A swallow soars in by the south door,
traces high rafters. Open sky.
The time it takes to pass through the north door,
span   of a life.

I am in love with the kinglet lost from its migrating flock
     who spins an airy path,
         pecan tree to reflecting glass, manic tap of a beak,
         red-feathered head flashing November sun.
This morning, still, at my bedroom window—
the cat stretches on the sill
watching a small bird looking   for itself.

Dia de Los Muertos at Mission Park Cemetery—
     Mama and I speak with Grandma in her grave—
     San Antonio light spikes across waxwings
     roosting in cedars, trees of the dead.

1896–1986.   Symmetry in numbers, balance of a life—
ridiculous chrysanthemums in a pock-marked urn.
Mama cries. I rise   like a note.

Dash on a headstone,
         space between the birth of light
         and the night when a spirit flew.
Standing here, who will know the stories?
The grandmother, who lived like a hummingbird—
drunk   in a hot pink ocean of penta flowers.

November in Texas: mockingbirds shove
         between branches of persimmon trees—
         snatching the orange globes.
Outside, beyond the acrid noise of pecans
on metal roofs, a flat cerulean sky, the unbroken
blue.   This cannot last.

A station wagon packed with kids—southside—
         rag-quilts for naps under trees—fried chicken,
         sugared cookies shaped like marks on a deck of cards—
         food we don't know we won't eat when we're old.
Laughing in late fall, we chase doves on a leafy bank
of the river where grandmother wades
in afternoon light   looking for fish.

The day you died, a white bird
         drifted in my kitchen, circled, swept away
         into night; my bones wept for a whispered *come with me*
         but the spirit sang *stay.*   *I am here with you.*
We will drink red wine under turning trees, remember
leaning back-to-back on October porches, laughing,
dreaming of being beautifully old, faces lit—
chrysanthemum explosions on the west wall.

At the end

of a morning walk, persimmon
skin—brave new light—

a tree at the green margin
of the garden calls

a quiet bell-song—
shining orbs.

Drawn to feed
I reach inside

grasp a red-orange
persimmon swelling

in shadows. My sudden
movement—startles

a bird, who flutters—
settles near—stares

at me, not wondering
why I'm here.

Listening to Bach's Art of Fugue

For Roberto Bonazzi

I.

I am sand at the edge of moon.

A body unmoored
moving at the whim
of moon.

And we don't know the rest of the story.

Like salt, the sea—
the sea, like salt.

II.

Weaving water and space
the size of loss.

Come.
Lie down and stare at sky
—waves move
over our bodies—
a creator blessing a birth.

III.

This is not sorrow,
not grief—
not even death,
but the border between
today
and tomorrow—

the line that divides
life
from longing.

Like a dream where you try
hard as you can
to run—and silence muffles screams.

You raise your hands
to shut silence out—
stand on the bridge between past
and present—mouth round
in fear of a future.

IV.

We lie on a beach, not on dry sand,
but on the damp part at the end
of land—where our eyes watch
a world under the one we know.

Let's settle into the shift of it,
feel the suck at our roots, water
moving below the surface.

Fall in the Hill Country

*Oh, you know now how wrong
they were, the philosophers.*

It is the edge of morning when,
if you go out, you feel you are interrupting
a sacred act, creation maybe,
one of the days before humans bloomed
in a perfect garden.

You push open the cabin door,
see light rush among live oaks,
a herd of green horses
stamping their hooves in the spirit world.

The field beyond is pulsing
with something more than words,
alone in its rock-strewn beauty
except for one old maple
stirring in wind across early sky

like a yellow river fluent
over burnt gold stones—
inhabits the world
the way you long to.

Spelling

At ten, I'd never heard the word—
so when, at the San Antonio spelling bee
the man pronounced my final round

I had no way to sound it out—
only one syllable—poor word
in a poor girl's mouth.

It was 50/50, I knew that much:
dirth with an *I*, dirth like *dirt*—
or dearth like *earth*, which is also dirt.

In the end, I went with dirt
and lost my faith in luck.

At ten, I knew, you could study and pray
—prepare for ambitious,
loquacious, even extraneous—

and then out of nowhere—get
a one-syllable test,
a word close to death—

And all you can do is smile
and try to spell.

Bones

I remember my head full,
so full of moonlight the brain blooms

and sails, a ship in a bottle—
the feel of feet kicking
out of my eyes.

Having been young once,
I think it is too much
to embrace maturity
with one dumb face.

I will let my body carve
a path through the air—my head

a blue parrot riding
the cool back of a rattler.

A thousand years away,
I will be the bones

some anthropologist holds
up to the light, amazed

by the music they make.

When Absence is Presence

Circle of sunlit grass, sleeping deer
if you know what you see.
Fat caterpillar on a leafless stem.
Scat on the path to the river, feathers
tracing the wake of coyote's raid.

Hunger for the voice
                of the dead.
Arc of ripples from a flat stone,
and the memory of a young arm's
                flash in the sun.

Our present life. The outer layer
of a tree; fused to spiraling
breathing past.

Like the fountain in the wall of La Mansion
I observe again, today, from a window.

Yesterday I watched
a teen-aged brown couple with two children—
baby in a stroller rocked by a boy-like man
wearing a sideways baseball cap, baggy pants
barely hanging on;

a round mother lifts
the toddler into the basin,
patiently bathes his feet,
his face in the late
afternoon heat.

Joy

It is loud, like god laughing.
Thunder, when a drought
has gone on too long.

The fire you build after rain.

Does it ride in on sound—
purple martins you hear
on a dim February morning?

Or the cry of the baby you were told
you'd never have, born
healthy in your middle age?

Its dimensions, delicate
—the gradual lengthening of days,

or the first faint-colored light
of dawn—like forgiveness
or cessation of pain—

Inherited—like family—
straight hair, fragile skin,
a grandmother's bold stare.

Or does it fall on you?
A kind of grace—

like a name that fits—
like luck, like faith.

Distances

Here, huisache—yellow,
thorny bouganvillea erupts in fuschia.
Plumbago and esperanza to trim,
tomato seeds to plant, thin blades of bulbs
to water; mulch to protect petunias and marigolds
from predators and drought.

Hands ushering in
a new season.

Easy to forget, this time of year,
death we launched with wars far away
from here. Hard to be a Breughel
holding two worlds in the same frame.

We are all farmers, like the one
in the famous painting who plowed
his fields in sun—

or the shepherd focused on his flock
chewing grass near the edge of a cliff—

or the fisherman leaning close
over the water to check his line—

while Icarus plunges into the sea
and drowns.

My Last Lithuanian Aunt

For Mary Louisa

It's good the light shines in my house.
No shadows left from the life
she had—before death took its place.

Or in the breath of God that heaves
in the hymn I sing alone.

I bend to light
the fire while a thousand
miles away, they lower
the bones, flesh resting
in frozen ground.

    I hear her loud laugh.
    The deep sigh
    as she eats
    potatoes; every day
    more potatoes: *a real Lithuanian,*

    she laughs. Today, I hold her stories,
    the only Lithuanian woman left
    to gather—the words.

Here on this table, daffodils
yellow at noon—
sun streaming through south-
facing windows.

San Antonio Summer

1.

Before the rain, just before the rain—
a hummingbird lingers at the red mouth
of August. A south wind moves
silver-green sycamore leaves—bees
and butterflies on hot pink penta clusters.
Ginger blooms in high sun; gold esperanza
full against the chain-link fence.

Storm-clouds in from the west—
metal-roof, watery-notes play orange
hibiscus music, riff on yellow lantana,
wash over gardenias and blue
plumbagos, as they push down the drive
to Mission Street—rush south
to the river.

2.

*Trapped sixty years in this dead place,
never dreamed. No real trees. Goddamn sun.
Survived a seven-year drought. The 50's.
Damned if I won't spend the rest of my life
in one.* Ignoring the frown on my face,
he explains: *Eighty-three now, might make ninety—
that's seven years before I die.*

This morning, rain spills over the gutter,
splashes off ginger, ripples
down bricks on its way to the river.
I phone my Daddy
a few miles away, ask if it's raining—
though I know it's not.

The Painting

Somehow over the years,
it disappeared, maybe after
he sobered up,
or when Mama, in a fit, cast out
evidence of a past
she preferred to erase—

the only thing we ever had on a wall
besides kids' drawings in the kitchen
and dead chrysantheum corsages festooned
with high school football game ribbons
in our teenage-boyfriend bedroom.

It hung for years over the couch—
frameless, dark, brooding,
like a Turner without education,
a storm on water, no land
in sight, no boat.

The only painting I ever did, he said.
Five children and a wife
working to pay the bills; how
did he find money for paint,
brushes, particle board
and time—

I picture him alone in the dark
bedroom they shared, carved
from a one-car garage at the two-
bedroom house on Glamis Street.

Grandma's Daughter

Mama is the sunny one, in the middle—
wide open smile—slender

arms taut in the sleeveless flowered
shirt, fingers touching the top ruffle
of her double-tiered skirt. Although

the photo is black and white you know
the flowers are red or purple or rose.

Even her bobbed black hair
casting light, separates her
from grandma's *other* children.

Only her eyes betray her, falling
in shadows beneath dark

bangs—they travel the bus
from Victoria Courts to the night shift
at Santa Rosa, five kids

left alone at a home that can never
be a home—the handsome husband,

dimples flashing, blond hair
burning at the corner ice house.

Double Overtime

Movie-star looks and charm—
eighty-six now—ignored by half
his daughters, tolerated by
one son still seeking
an approving grin—
the one he saves for me.

My father huddles in his stained
armchair wearing two jackets
on this day in April when it's 78
degrees, his lanky frame

shrinking daily, waiting for his wife
of 62 years to return, cook klatskes,
kugele, anything to bring back the flavor
of Lithuania, the language he lost,

uprooted twice—from native land,
then Illinois coal-fields when
he followed Mama to Texas.

I try to imagine always wanting
what you won't have—to be someone
somewhere else, hear words no one
around you knows, children who speak
your language—and don't remember
everything. A life you can rewind

before vodka, before finding your mother
in bed with a stranger before
you and your twin sister walked in
hungry, home from school
where the teacher laughed
at your accent.

I touch his forehead,
assure him he has no fever,
escape into honeysuckled air—
drive home to watch
my team win
in double overtime
again.

Winter Roses

My feet whisper on the concrete walk,
the words *here* and *now*—as though they are
a new tongue in this old place—Pereida, South Presa, Alamo,
St. Mary's—a grid on a map that spells *home*.

A rooster crows, and again
        I am nine years old on the way to school
        snatching sticky gold kumquats
        off dark green trees, sucking sweet meat,
        spitting the shiny black seeds.
        Wiry tendrils on fences
        offer sweet-pea colors.
        And irises, huge purple ones, when I kneel to smell,
        leave a yellow blessing.
        But most of all, roses: spicy gold, heady pink, reds
        I steal from bush to bush, yard to yard
        on my way to Mama, afternoons,
        finding reasons to see her smile.

        The rooster belongs to someone's house
        on a street with a name, not Lindsay Walk
        where our building sits in Victoria Courts.
        Mama says, *Tell them you live on Lindsay,*
        never say Walk, poor people live on walks.

Drawn by roses on every block—
I am led this morning down Leigh Street.
Fragrant voices of winter roses—
heavy roses, fire-red clusters, flat-petal pinks
with golden mouths murmur,
It is never too cold here.

The Parakeet of Grief

When grief comes to you as a purple gorilla,
you must count yourself lucky.

— Matthew Dickman

No. Grief is a little friend, lavender. Pale blue. Less human
—a caged bird whose door you occasionally open—
unless he unlatches himself with a trained beak.

Like Burt, the pet parakeet I kept,
who perched on my shoulder as I worked—
washing dishes in the kitchen, looking down
at my hands in the sink, wrist-deep in water. Or staring
out the window counting on tomorrow. Who nestled inside
my collar as I curled in an armchair reading
stories to get through the days—clung to my thumb,
pecked crumbs from my palm, meant to be gentle—
delivered the inevitable wound.

Gone, I rarely thought of him. But at the door to my house—
he'd fly from his perch on the lampshade
in the closest corner, or the curtain rod on the far window—
If I failed to grant enough attention, he'd light
on my head. Quick wings tangled
fine strands—knots needing hours to smooth.

Four years, he kept me company—until
the night he made his final pass around the room—
flew into the back of grandma's rocker.

The bent neck—I called for help—a voice on the line—
nothing to do. Wrapping his body in blue cloth
—substance and hue, a slow loss—

I pushed a sharp shovel into the dirt,
a hole sufficiently deep.

Fishing: the Last Time

You promised to take him
every summer to the pond

in the woods near your house.
My son, only four, knew

you as his heart-aunt forever.
You promised to take him,

helped him thread
the worm on the hook,

swing the pole over
still water, your right arm

flashing brown in the sun.
You smiled at his serious

face, passed him the pole,
and the bait dangled

below. He stood still—
stared at the water,

hushing us
when we laughed.

White Light

The two of us sitting on the pine table
in the open field at the end
of the path

I dragged you down,
out of the log cabin you dreamed
into being. Almost sunset.
Not wanting to let you rest
in your porch chair, the furthest you'd gone
in weeks.

I half-carried you
down the dirt road
to the clearing. Wanting
you in my world
again.

We stopped for food you could not eat.
Leaning together on the warm
table top, I made you look
at dogwood blooming white light
in dense pines
at the edge. I spoke
about *next* spring—when
you would eat
again. We stayed too long,

had to call for help
to carry you back
to bed.

Your Baby's Grave

Rose White and Rose Red.
Wild women who ate men.
Survived paths cut with the same glass—
flew through the world, full
of wonder, witches on brooms.

Babies bloomed in our bellies
at the same late age—
same doctor, same tests,
same telephone call, different
message—

I would have my baby alone.

Mourning hid behind the face
you gave to me, the grace you grew
to welcome the baby
we would share.

So big I could barely bend.
You, so thin—we placed
the marker we carved
beneath the dogwood tree.

Spirit Bundle for Diane

> *Lakota people honor loved ones who have died by preparing a bundle. They stay with the spirit until they are ready to let it go.*
>
> — Ella Cara Deloria

        Sister,
I will keep you with me a while.
I have smoothed your magenta scarf, spread
the silk
        a lock of chestnut hair folded in a leaf
        of paper you sent long ago.
        You wrote just one word. *Mim.*
        —signed with only the letter *D*;
        the white space before
        my eyes bloomed
        like a desert flower after
        rain, a rich and silent language.

        Here is the turquoise elephant I brought
        you from Chiang Mai—
        and your lapis stones, diamonds for those
        who love color more than light.
        The book of poems you marked
        with a blue jay feather, writing in the margins,
        Look at the man who sings to animals
        who sleeps smiling in the jungle
        while we, in narrow beds, dream
        of falling off cliffs and wake afraid.

I will bring you yellow roses, white irises
and cashew chicken—fried shrimp, garlic spinach,
things you loved but could not relish

at the end of this world. We will drink red wine
together and remember leaning back to back
against each other—laughing, dreaming of being
beautiful old ladies charming gray-haired men.

In the Mourning Store

I am shopping for death
unsure of what to choose—
the manner or when.

Between now and then
I want to clothe
myself appropriately—classic black
perhaps—thousands of widows
of history.

I must dress
for a journey
through the islands
of mourning.

It is work to die.
Or to witness the universal
massacre.

Death, like life, requires
participation—response.

In my ritual of witness,
it is life that haunts—
this morning sun
lighting the high tips
of the fuschia bougainvillea
pushing through
the south fence,
the hummingbird at the window,
cinnamon coffee—

what awaits
when I return.

The Birds' Journey

> *... and after us there will be a horizon for the new birds.*
>
> — Mahmoud Darwish (1941-2008)

1.

Sky. Slopes. Road.
Carving light-words into the true *heart*
*of darkne*s. Soulsoaked path where plants grow

because you watered their roots. Above
the lush road—birds,
new birds—as long as you attend

to the work—create a road lit,
build a road green
and wide under a dependable sky—

after you've reddened with blood
the stone—
sky raucous with journeys of new birds

calling—*Long live life*
as they fly the road
you walked into being.

2.

Birds flying far find it is all
one day
with constant light. Birds turning

into it—ancient graves hiding
—cerements still blue
in the dark—graves old and new

covered in patches of grass
or simple dirt
regularly turn into light.

3.

What the poet taught: we are all
part of healing
the world we've got.

What We Know Growing Up in South Texas

I know about huisache
how early spring branches swell
with yellow flowers the size of orange seeds,
how they breathe a fragrance into the warm world—
Makes me think about creation—
the moment when color and scent
exactly echoed the weather.

And the chinaberry I know
flaunts four seasons, like a woman who doesn't care
what they say about beauty:
how winter-grayed limbs hold dull clusters
up to a waning sky; unfurl March gold—
mauve flowers float down, leaving green
dark branches to burn butter-yellow
               come fall.

I know the backyard sycamore's
vigor—grows fast with you as silver bark splits
and curls against its smooth interior—
how you can read, leaning against its trunk, listen
to hand-shaped leaves, observe
their gray-green velvet undersides subtly
               mimic wind.

I know, too, about mesquite—
how when rain stays away for a while
the mesquite still sends out stiff thorns
and lacy wings. Fools us. We will wait
for the water that will return
whether we are here—or not.

About the Author

Marian Aitches is a native of San Antonio, Texas, where she grew up in Victoria Courts, one of the country's oldest subsidized public housing projects. She graduated from Highlands High School and San Antonio Community College before going on to receive her Ph.D. from the University of North Texas in 1990.

An award-winning professor, she is currently a senior lecturer in the department of History at the University of Texas at San Antonio. She teaches courses focusing on American Indian studies, as well as race, ethnicity, gender and class. *Fishing for Light* is her first book of poetry.

Acknowledgments

"Bones" and "Spelling" first appeared in *The Texas Monthly*.

"Spirit Bundle for Diane" first appeared in the anthology *150 Poems of Grief and Gratitude* (Holy Cow Press).

I would like to thank my colleagues and friends: Bonnie Lyons, who started me writing morning pages; Cyra Dumitru, my first poetry teacher; Naomi Shihab Nye and Roberto Bonazzi, who believed in my work; the Wild-Eyed Tribe, who faithfully responded to my words; the Mamas group, who kept me laughing; and my friends Lila Walker, Ruth Ann Gambino, and Jan Davis, who call me a poet. Greatest gratitude goes to Marian Haddad, enthusiastic audience, mentor and friend—mi tocaya.

None of this would matter without the love and support of the two men in my life—Mel Laracey and our son, Nicolas.

Five hundred copies of

Fishing for Light

have been numbered and signed

by the author.

Marian Aitches

This is number _179_

April 2009

Wings Press
Whitebird Chapbook Series
Number 4

Colophon

Five hundred copies of the first edition of *Fishing for Light*, by Marian Aitches, have been printed on 70 pound paper containing fifty percent recycled fiber. Titles have been set in Papyrus type, the text in Adobe Caslon type. All Wings Press books are designed and produced by Bryce Milligan.

This chapbook series is named in honor of Joanie Whitebird, founder of Wings Press. As *The Texas Observer* described her, Joanie was "an old-fashioned fence hater, a wire-cutter, a woman in love with the open road, with open relationships, with open futures fraught with possibilities." We honor her spirit by using this series to introduce new and innovative poetic voices.

www.wingspress.com

Wings Press titles are distributed
to the trade by the
Independent Publishers Group
www.ipgbook.com